Contents

The Birth of the Prophet Muhammad

In the year 570CE, the Prophet Muhammad, peace be upon him, was born in Makkah, a city in Saudi Arabia. His father, Abdullah, died a few months before his birth. His mother's name was Amina. Amina was good and pretty and pure, and Allah, the One God, had chosen her to be Muhammad's mother. The happy news was proclaimed far and wide, in the heavens and on Earth. Soft breezes blew, crops grew lush and green, and trees bowed under the weight of their fruit. The whole world was filled with joy.

A few days before the Prophet's birth, an angel appeared from the sky and visited Amina in her dreams.

"I bring you good news," the angel said. "Oh mother of the blessed last prophet. Your son will be the lord of the worlds, the best of men. He will save the world. When he is born, you must say these words, 'I place him under Allah's protection, safe from wickedness and envy.' And you must call him Muhammad, the praised one."

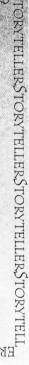

Did you know?

Muslims believe that Allah has sent many prophets to teach people how to live. Muhammad was the last and greatest of these prophets. Among the prophets that came before him were Adam, Nuh (Noah), Ibrahim (Abraham), Musa (Moses) and Isa (Jesus). They are also important figures in Judaism and Christianity. Muslims often write the letters 'pbuh' after the names of the prophets. These stand for the words 'peace be upon him'.

STORYTELLER: ISLAMIC STORIES

Anita Ganeri

Illustrations by Rebecca Wallis

Evans

EVANS BROTHERS LIMITED

Introduction

Islamic Stories

 n each of the world's six main religions - Hinduism, Judaism, Buddhism, Christianity, Islam and Sikhism - stories play a very important part. They have been used for many hundreds of years to teach people about their faith in a way which makes difficult messages easier to understand. Many stories tell of times in the lives of religious teachers, leaders, gods and goddesses. Others explain mysterious events such as how the world was created or what happens when you die. Many have a strong moral or lesson to teach.

he collection of stories in this book comes from Islam. Islam is the religion followed by Muslims. They believe in one God, whom they call Allah. They follow Allah's guidance throughout their lives. Islam began in the 7th century CE in the country we now call Saudi Arabia in the Middle East. A man called Muhammad was chosen by Allah to receive his message for the world. He was the last of all the prophets of Islam. The messages were later collected together to make the Qur'an, the Muslim holy book. Allah did not speak to Muhammad directly. His messenger was an angel called Jibril. In this book, you can read some of the stories which show how Allah gave His message to the world through His angels and prophets.

Muhammad was born just before daybreak on a Monday, on the thirteenth day of the month of Rabbi-ul-Awwal, in the year of the Elephant. It is said that many strange and miraculous things happened at the time of his birth. The stars in the sky glowed more brightly and a brilliant light shone, bright enough to light up the whole world. Muhammad's face appeared in the full Moon. All these were signs that Allah had chosen Muhammad to be His blessed last prophet and to bring His message to the world. After his birth, his grandfather took him to the sacred Ka'bah shrine in Makkah to pray to Allah and thank Him for this precious gift.

As a young baby, Muhammad was cared for by his foster mother, Halima, and brought up with her own little son. Along with many other women, Halima had travelled to Makkah to look for a baby to nurse. This was the custom at that time. When she saw Muhammad, she felt sad for him. No other woman wanted to nurse ▶

him because he did not have a father. Now Halima was poor but she was also kind-hearted. She took Muhammad to live in her house. And her kindness was rewarded. For while Muhammad lived with Halima, her fortunes changed and Allah blessed her life. She had plenty of food to feed her family, her sheep and camels thrived, and her date trees blossomed.

Muhammad grew up to be healthy and strong. But when he was just six years old, tragedy struck. His mother, Amina, fell ill

and died, leaving Muhammad an orphan. The little boy went to live with his grandfather, then with his uncle, Abu Talib, a wealthy merchant, who cared for him as his own son. He knew that his nephew was no ordinary person and that great things lay in store for him. Muhammad grew up to be kind, thoughtful and hard-working, and was loved and trusted by everyone. He was known as someone who never broke his word. That is why he was called 'al-Amin', which means 'the truthful one'.

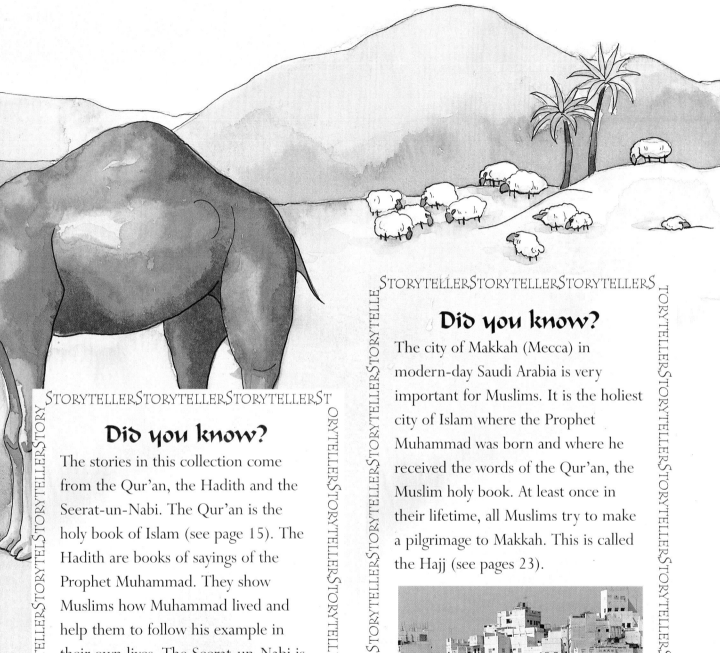

STORYTELLERSTORYTELLERSTORYTELLERST

Did you know?

The stories in this collection come from the Qur'an, the Hadith and the Seerat-un-Nabi. The Qur'an is the holy book of Islam (see page 15). The Hadith are books of sayings of the Prophet Muhammad. They show Muslims how Muhammad lived and help them to follow his example in their own lives. The Seerat-un-Nabi is the story of Muhammad's life, written by a man called Ibn-e-Ishaq. He wrote the first biography of Muhammad. Some Muslims do not agree with the tales he tells about miracles but his writing is mostly well respected.

Did you know?

The city of Makkah (Mecca) in modern-day Saudi Arabia is very important for Muslims. It is the holiest city of Islam where the Prophet Muhammad was born and where he received the words of the Qur'an, the Muslim holy book. At least once in their lifetime, all Muslims try to make a pilgrimage to Makkah. This is called the Hajj (see pages 23).

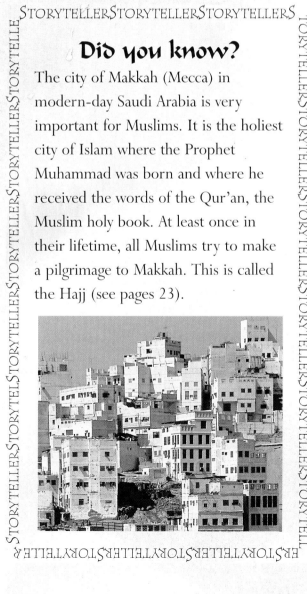

The Cleansing of the Heart

According to legend, a very strange and extraordinary thing happened while Muhammad was living with Halima. One day, Muhammad was playing with his friends in the fields at the back of Halima's house, when all of a sudden two angels, dressed in dazzling white, came walking towards him. One was carrying a silver jug; the other a golden platter, piled high with snow. The two angels grabbed hold of Muhammad's arms. One angel held him tightly, while the other took out a sharp knife. He cut open Muhammad's chest, and took out the boy's heart. Though Muhammad could see what was happening, he did not feel any pain. Then the angel took a black speck from Muhammad's heart

STORYTELLERSTORYTELLERSTORYTELLERS

Did you know?

Muslims follow five duties, called the five pillars of Islam. They support Islam, just as real pillars support a building. The first pillar is the Shahadah. This is a sentence which sums up what Muslims believe. It says: "There is no other God but Allah and Muhammad is His Prophet." The other pillars are prayer (see page 18), giving alms to the poor, fasting at Ramadan (see page 15) and making the Hajj pilgrimage to Makkah (see page 23).

and threw it far away. He washed the heart thoroughly in snow, to make it pure, and placed it back into the boy's body.

heavier, worth more than a hundred others.

"Weigh him against a thousand people," the angel said.

And they weighed him, and he was heavier, worth more than a thousand others. Then the angels went away. When they were gone, Halima, Muhammad's foster-mother, came running up to find him. His friends had told her what had happened. To her relief, she found Muhammad safe and sound, although something about him, she could not quite tell what it was, had well and truly changed.

Did you know?

Many Muslims believe that this story shows how Allah made Muhammad pure and clean, ready to receive His message. The black speck, which the angel took from his heart, stands for the devil's evil powers. Many other strange and wonderful events are said to have happened around the time of Muhammad's birth and childhood. They show that Muhammad was a very special person.

Then the angel said, "Weigh him against a hundred people."

And they weighed him, and he was

The First Revelations

When Muhammad left Halima's house, he went to live in Makkah, first with his grandfather, then with his uncle, Abu Talib. He worked hard as a shepherd, then as a merchant, learning his trade from Abu Talib. When he was 25 years old, he went to work for a rich and noble widow called Khadijah who was also a merchant in Makkah. Now Khadijah was not only wealthy, she was honourable, wise and respected as well. She was so impressed by Muhammad's honesty and truthfulness that she sent him a proposal of marriage. Muhammad asked his uncle for his blessing. In great delight, Abu Talib agreed to the match.

For many years, Muhammad lived happily in Makkah. He loved his wife and his business did very well. But he also saw how much greed and cruelty there was in the world, particularly towards people who were less well off. Muhammad began to spend more time by himself, in prayer and meditation, trying to work out how to make things better. Sometimes he was away from home for days, staying in a cave on nearby Mount Hira, the mountain of light, and living off water, dried bread and dates. Sometimes he heard voices saying,

"Peace be on you, O Messenger of God!"

But when he looked for the speaker, there was no one there.

One day, when Muhammad was praying on Mount Hira, an amazing thing happened. A dazzling light filled the cave and a shadowy figure of an angel appeared before him. The figure held out a piece of cloth which was covered in writing.

"Read!" the figure told Muhammad.

"I cannot read," Muhammad replied. He had never learnt how to read or write.

Twice more the voice commanded him.

"Read!" the voice said.

Suddenly, Muhammad found that he could read the words and knew what they said. He felt as if the words had always been with him, written on his heart. He spoke the words out loud:

"Recite! In the name of your Lord who created all people from a drop of blood.

Recite! Your Lord is the most generous one who taught people by the pen what they did not know."

Muhammad rushed from the cave and started to run down the mountain side. Then he heard a voice, calling to him:

"O Muhammad, do not be afraid. You are Allah's messenger, and I am the angel, Jibril."

Muhammad turned and saw the mysterious figure who had spoken to him in the cave. He raced home, shaking with fear, and told Khadijah what had happened. She comforted him and reassured him, for she knew in her heart that what the angel had said was true.

Muhammad was about 40 years old. From that moment on, his life changed forever. He had been called to be Allah's prophet and to spend the rest of his life in Allah's service, teaching people how Allah wanted them to live. The way of life he taught was called Islam, which means 'obeying Allah's will'. His first followers were his wife, Khadijah, his nephew, Ali, and his friend, Abu Bakr, the merchant. ▶

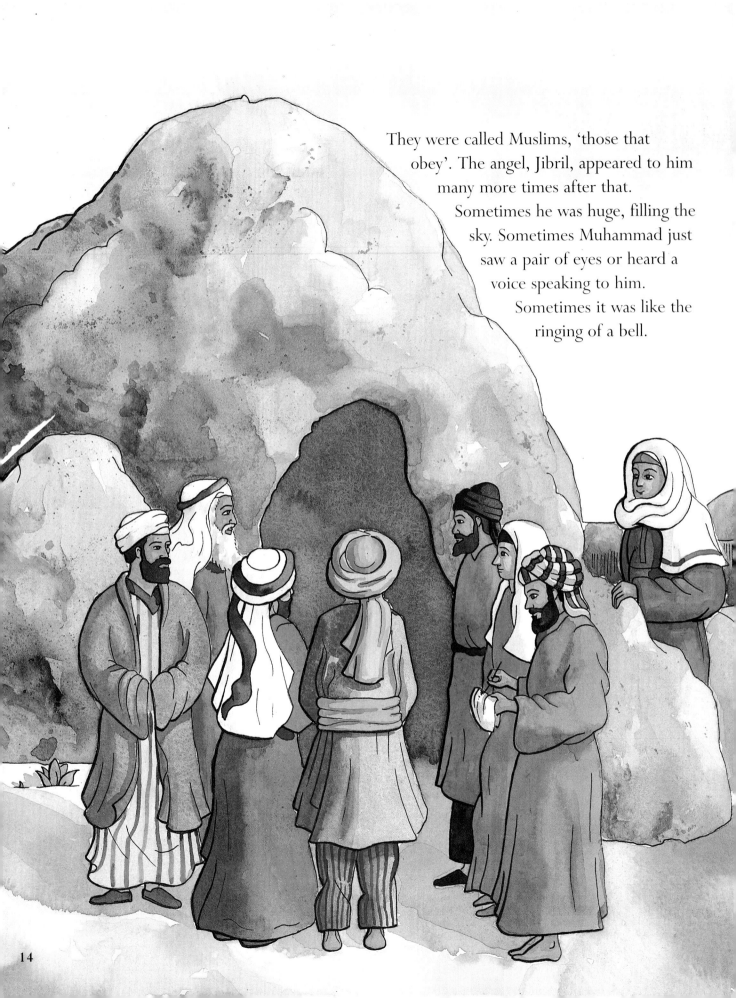

They were called Muslims, 'those that obey'. The angel, Jibril, appeared to him many more times after that.
Sometimes he was huge, filling the sky. Sometimes Muhammad just saw a pair of eyes or heard a voice speaking to him.
Sometimes it was like the ringing of a bell.

The messages he brought came from Allah in words that Muhammad recited to his friends. Some of these friends wrote the words down at the time to keep them forever. Later, they were collected to become the holy Qur'an.

Did you know?

Ramadan is the ninth month of the Islamic calendar. This is the month when the Qur'an was first revealed to the Prophet Muhammad by Jibril. It is also the month when Muslims fast between sunrise and sunset. Fasting is the fourth pillar of Islam. It helps to teach self-control and compassion for others. The end of Ramadan is marked by the happy festival of Id-ul-Fitr.

Did you know?

The Qur'an is the holy book of Islam. Muslims treat the Qur'an with great honour because they believe that it contains the exact words of Allah and His message for the world. These words were revealed, or given, to Muhammad by the angel, Jibril. Muslims use the Qur'an as the guide for their lives. Reading, reciting and studying the Qur'an is a very important duty for Muslims.

Did you know?

Muslims believe that angels are heavenly beings who carry messages between Allah and Earth because it is not fitting for Allah to speak directly to people. Angels are created by Allah, out of light. They are usually invisible but can take any shape they wish. One of the most important angels is Jibril, or Gabriel. He brings Allah's message to the prophets. He sometimes appeared to Muhammad in human form.

The Night of the Journey

One night, as Muhammad was sleeping near the holy mosque in Makkah, the angel Jibril came to the Prophet and woke him up. He had come to take Muhammad on an amazing journey. Jibril led the Prophet to the gate of the mosque, where there stood a fabulous beast called Buraq, or Lightning. As white as snow, with a horse's body, it had two great wings on its back. Jibril lifted the Prophet on to Buraq's back, and together, they sped through the skies to the city of Jerusalem. There Muhammad met Ibrahim and Musa, and the other prophets who had come before him, and led them in prayer.

Then Jibril brought him two goblets, one full of wine and the other of milk. Muhammad drank the goblet of milk but did not touch the wine.

"You must teach your people to do the same," Jibril said. "For Muslims are forbidden to drink wine."

But the night of the journey was not yet over. Jibril showed Muhammad a beautiful ladder of silver and gold, and told him to climb up it. Up they climbed, until they reached one of the gates of heaven, called the Gate of the Keepers. There, twelve thousand angels stood guard.

"Is this the true Prophet?" an angel said.

"It is," replied Jibril.

Together they passed through the gate and up through the seven heavens. In each of the heavens, Muhammad met the prophets who had come before him, among them Adam, Isa, Musa and Ibrahim. In each of the heavens, Jibril was asked:

"Who is this, O Jibril?"

"Muhammad, the Prophet," Jibril replied.

At last, they reached the seventh heaven and the Prophet entered Paradise where he came before the Throne of God, into Allah's glorious presence. There Allah gave the commandment to Muhammad that all Muslims should pray fifty times a day.

On Muhammad's way back down to Earth, he once again met Musa.

"How many times must you pray?" Musa asked.

"Fifty times a day," said the Prophet.

"Prayer is a heavy burden," Musa said. "And people are weak and lazy. Go back to your Lord and ask him to make the number of prayers less."

So Muhammad returned to the highest heaven and asked Allah to reduce the number of prayers. Ten prayers were taken off. But still Musa repeated his warning, and several times more Muhammad returned to Allah and asked Him to make the number of prayers less. Soon so many prayers had been taken off that only five were left. Muhammad could not go back and ask for fewer than that. ▶

Did you know?

In the Qur'an, heaven, or Paradise, is described as a beautiful garden where birds sing, flowers bloom, the soil smells sweet and the rocks are made from gold and jewels. Muslims believe that people who follow Allah faithfully will go to Paradise when they die. The punishment for a wicked or sinful life is to be sent to Hell.

Did you know?

The Dome of the Rock is a beautiful mosque in Jerusalem, built between 688-691CE. After Makkah and Madinah (Medina), it is the third holiest place in Islam. Inside the mosque is the holy rock from which Muslims believe Muhammad made his Night Journey into heaven.

"Whoever says his prayers faithfully five times a day," he said, "shall have the same rewards as for fifty."

Then, before a new day dawned, Muhammad mounted Buraq again and flew back to Makkah. It is said that his bed was still warm, just as he had left it.

Did you know?

Prayer, or Salaat, is the second pillar of Islam. Muslims pray five times a day, as Allah instructed Muhammad. They pray at dawn, midday, mid-afternoon, sunset and at night. Muslims must face towards Makkah as they pray. In a mosque, a special arch in the wall shows the right direction. Before they pray, they wash their hands, feet and face to make them fit to talk to Allah.

Musa Follows a Wise Man

Once the Prophet Musa (Moses) was travelling back from the land where the two seas meet when he came upon a wise man. This man was a true servant of Allah, to whom Allah had given His mercy and the precious gift of knowledge.

"May I follow you," Musa said to the wise man, "so that you can teach me what you know?"

"You will not have the patience to follow me," replied the wise man.

"I promise to be patient," said Musa. "And to obey whatever you say. If only you will let me go with you."

"Very well," said the wise man. "You may come. But you must not ask any questions. I will tell you about things when I am ready."

Musa agreed to do as the wise man said, and the two set out on the journey. Very soon afterwards, they came to a ship. The wise man bored a hole in the ship's bottom.

"Why did you do that?" Musa asked, in astonishment. "Do you want the ship's passengers to drown?"

"Didn't I tell you that you would lose patience?" replied the wise man. Immediately, Musa apologised for his forgetfulness and asked the wise man not to be angry.

Next, the two met a young man, whom the wise man killed. ▶

"Why have you killed an innocent man?" Musa exclaimed in horror. "That was a wicked and terrible thing to do!"

"Didn't I tell you that you would lose patience?" said the wise man again, and again Musa apologised.

"If I ever question you again," he said, "leave me behind. I shall have deserved it."

Musa and the wise man travelled on their way until they reached a city. They asked its people for food and shelter but no one would help them. As they left the city, they saw a wall which was falling down and the wise man stopped to mend it.

"Why didn't you ask for some payment in return?" asked Musa. "You could have if you'd wanted to."

"The time has come," the wise man replied, "for us to part company. But first I will explain my actions to you. The ship we saw belonged to some poor fishermen. But a king wanted to take it from them. The fishermen can easily mend the hole I bored but it makes the ship useless to the king."

"As for the young man," the wise man continued, "his death spared his parents a lifetime of misery. They will have another son who will love them and look after them."

"As for the wall, it belonged to two city orphans whose father was a good man. Treasure is buried beneath it. It is Allah's will that, when they grow up, they will dig the treasure up. Now you know why I acted as I did. It was not my will but Allah's."

The Story of Ibrahim and Isma'il

The Prophet Ibrahim (Abraham) was known as the Friend of Allah. Although he was a wealthy man, he was also humble and devout, and had vowed to dedicate his life to Allah and everything dear to Him. He lived peacefully with his two wives, Sara and Hajra, and his son, Isma'il, whom he loved very much. The Qur'an tells the story of Ibrahim and Isma'il.

One night, Ibrahim had a dream. He dreamt that Allah wanted him to sacrifice his most precious possession, his beloved son, Isma'il. Now Isma'il was just ten years old but Ibrahim went to find him and told him his dream.

"Father, we must do as Allah wishes," Isma'il said.

So Ibrahim took Isma'il to Mina, near the holy city of Makkah, to carry out Allah's wishes. On the way, their path was blocked by a sinister stranger, the devil himself in disguise.

"Where are you going?" the stranger said to them.

"To carry out Allah's wishes," Ibrahim replied.

"But surely Allah would not wish you to kill your son," said the stranger. "That must be the work of the devil. Go home, and forget all about it."

Then Ibrahim recognised the stranger for who he was and continued on his way. Next, the devil tried to tempt Isma'il.

"Did you know that your father is planning to kill you?" he asked the boy.

"He must do as Allah commands," Isma'il replied. ▶

A third time, the devil tried to stop them carrying out Allah's wishes. He went to Hajra, Isma'il's mother, but she refused to listen. Then Isma'il and Ibrahim threw stones at the devil to drive him away.

Now it was time for the greatest test, time for Ibrahim to sacrifice his son. Isma'il lay face down on the ground, so that he could not see his father and put him off his task. Then Ibrahim took his knife, sharpened it and was just about to cut Isma'il's throat, when the knife was twisted from his hand and he heard Allah's voice calling to him:

"O Ibrahim, do not kill your son," the voice said. "You have already shown your love and obedience to me. Sacrifice this ram instead of Isma'il."

So, Ibrahim and Isma'il caught the ram which Allah had sent and sacrificed it instead, as Allah had commanded

Did you know?

Hajj begins and ends at the Ka'bah in Makkah. This is a cube-shaped shrine which Muslims believe was built by Ibrahim and Isma'il as a place for people to worship Allah. Every pilgrim walks around the Ka'bah seven times at the start and finish of Hajj.

Did you know?

Performing Hajj, the pilgrimage to Makkah, is the fifth pillar of Islam. When they arrive in Makkah, pilgrims change into simple, white clothes to show that all Muslims are equal. Then they visit various holy sites in and around Makkah. These include a place called Mina where they remember the story of Ibrahim and Isma'il. The pilgrims throw stones at three stone pillars which stand for the devil. They also celebrate the festival of Id-ul-Adha by sacrificing a sheep or goat.

The Story of Hajra

The Qur'an tells another story about Ibrahim. Once, long ago, Allah spoke again to Ibrahim. He told him to take Hajra, his wife, and Isma'il, his young son, out to the desert and to leave them there. As always, Ibrahim obeyed Allah's command. He left Hajra and Isma'il alone in the desert with only some dates and water.

"Why are you doing this?" Hajra asked.

"Because Allah wishes me to," replied Ibrahim.

Soon afterwards, the water ran out and there was nowhere to shelter from the baking heat. Hajra and Isma'il were very thirsty. But where could Hajra find water in the desert?

Everywhere she looked was dusty and dry. Perhaps there would be water in the nearby hills? So Hajra left Isma'il behind and walked from one hill to the other, back and forth, back and forth, but no water could she find. Whatever would they do?

Then she heard a voice calling to her, and she saw the angel, Jibril, standing close by. The angel was pointing at Isma'il.

Suddenly, Hajra saw water gushing up

Did you know?

On Hajj, pilgrims remember Hajra's story. After visiting the Ka'bah, they go to drink from the ancient well of Zamzam. Then they follow Hajra's path between the two hills of Al-Safa and Al-Marwa. But they do not have to walk through the baking desert as Hajra did. A long, modern building runs between the two hills. Pilgrims can walk up and down, or go by escalator.

out of the earth around Isma'il's feet. There was all the water she and Isma'il could drink. Allah had provided for them. This spring became known as Zamzam and its fame spread far and wide.

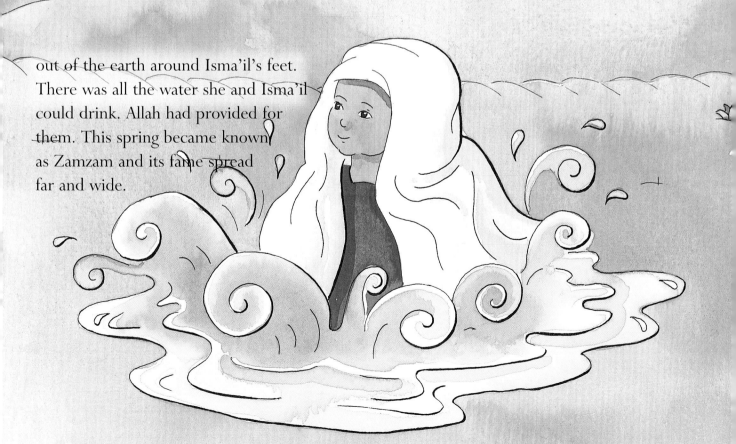

25

The Prophet Escapes to Madinah

For many years, the Prophet Muhammad lived in Makkah, the city of his birth. Here he began to teach people to follow the word of Allah and to accept Islam. At first, he taught only his friends and family, but many people came to hear him and listened carefully to what he said. Many followed him and became Muslims. But some people in Makkah did not like his message. The rich merchants were afraid of losing their power if people began to follow Muhammad's God. They offered him bribes to stop his preaching but Muhammad would not give up. Allah told Muhammad to leave for the city of Madinah, where he and his followers would be safe.

But the rich merchants of Makkah were secretly plotting to kill Muhammad before he could leave.

"We'll kill him early in the morning when he leaves his house to go to pray," they said.

But the angel, Jibril, appeared to Muhammad in his sleep and warned him of their wicked plot. The Prophet asked his cousin, Ali, to sleep in his house instead of him with Muhammad's cloak over him. He promised that Ali would come to no harm.

Then he, and his friend, Abu Bakr, made their getaway. They climbed on the backs of two swift camels and set off across the desert to Madinah. When the merchants found out that they had been tricked, they were furious. They offered a reward of one hundred camels to anyone who would bring them back. Then, they and their men set off after them.

The Prophet and Abu Bakr tried once again to fool their enemies, by riding south instead of north. But still they came after them. All night they rode on through the desert. Then, when day dawned, they found a cool mountain cave to shelter from the heat. Hot on their heels came the merchants and their men.

"Whatever shall we do?" asked Abu Bakr. "They're getting closer and are sure to see the entrance of the cave."

"Allah will protect us," Muhammad calmly replied.

And this is what happened. The men drew closer and closer, until they stood at the entrance of the cave. Muhammad and Abu Bakr could clearly hear their voices.

"Look!" one voice said. "A cave. They must be in there." ▶

"Don't be silly," another voice said. "No one's been into this cave for years. It's got a huge spider's web right across the entrance, and there's a dove sitting on its nest. No one's been near here, that's for sure."

Then the men went away. When at last Abu Bakr was sure they had gone, he turned to the Prophet.

"Where did the dove and the spider's web come from?" he asked. "They weren't here when we came in."

The Prophet smiled. Allah had protected them, as he knew He would.

A few days later, when at last it was safe to leave the cave, they continued their desert journey to Madinah where they received a very warm welcome. When they reached the city, Muhammad's camel stopped by a place where the dates were laid out to dry, and here the Prophet built the first mosque.

Did you know?

Muhammad's journey from Makkah to Madinah is known as the hijrah, or 'flight'. It took place in the year 622CE. This date marks the start of the Islamic calendar. The letters 'AH' are written after Muslim years to mean 'the year of the hijrah'. The Prophet died in Madinah in 632CE.

Did you know?

Today, there are more than a thousand million Muslims all over the world and Islam is the fastest-growing religion. Most Muslims live in the Middle East, Asia and Africa, in countries where Islam is the official religion. Although all Muslims share the same basic beliefs, there are several different groups. The largest groups are called the Sunni and the Shi'a. The worldwide family of Muslims is called the 'Ummah' or community.

Glossary

Abu Bakr A close friend of Muhammad. He accompanied Muhammad on his flight from Makkah to Madinah.

Allah The Islamic name for God.

Angels Heavenly beings who carry messages between Allah and people on earth.

Biography An account of a person's life story.

Dome of the Rock A mosque in Jerusalem. Inside is the sacred rock from which Muslims believe that Muhammad made his Night Journey.

Five pillars Five duties which Muslims follow in their lives.

Hadith Books of sayings of the Prophet Muhammad. Muslims use them as guides in their own lives.

Hajj The pilgrimage to Makkah which all Muslims try to make at least once in their lives.

Hijrah The name Muslims give to Muhammad's flight from Makkah to Madinah. The word 'Hijrah' means 'departure'.

Ibrahim A great prophet of Islam. He is also called Abraham and known as the Friend of Allah.

Id-ul-Adha The festival at the end of the Hajj when Muslims remember how Ibrahim almost sacrificed his son for Allah.

Id-ul-Fitr The festival when Muslims celebrate the end of Ramadan.

Islam The religion of the Muslims. They believe in one God, called Allah, and follow his guidance in their lives.

Jerusalem A city in Israel and the place from which Muhammad made his Night Journey.

Jibril The angel sent by Allah to tell Muhammad the words of the holy Qur'an. He is also called Gabriel.

Ka'bah A cube-shaped shrine in Makkah. Muslims always turn to face the Ka'bah when they pray.

Khadijah Muhammad's wife.

Madinah (Medina) A city in Saudi Arabia where Muhammad died in 632AD and where he died. It is a holy city for Muslims.

Makkah (Mecca) A city in Saudi Arabia where Muhammad was born. It is the Muslims' holiest city.

Miracles Amazing or magical events which cannot be explained.

Mosque A building where Muslims meet and pray.

Muhammad The last and greatest prophet of Islam. Muslims believe that he was sent by Allah to teach people how to live. He received the words of the holy Qur'an from the angel Jibril.

Musa A great prophet of Islam. He is also known as Moses.

Muslims People who follow the religion of Islam.

Paradise The name used by Muslims for heaven.

Pilgrimage A special journey to a holy place.

Pbuh Short for 'peace be upon him'. Muslims write these letter after the prophets' names.

Prophet Someone chosen by Allah to speak to people about His wishes for the world.

Qur'an The Muslims' holy book.

Ramadan A month during which Muslims fast (do not eat) between sunrise and sunset each day.

Saudi Arabia A country in the Middle East where Muhammad lived and where Islam began.

Index